The Firebird

for Solo Piano

The Firebird

for Solo Piano

Complete Ballet

Igor Stravinsky

DOVER PUBLICATIONS, INC.
Mineola, New York

Bibliographical Note

This Dover edition, first published in 2006, is an unabridged republication of the work originally published by G. Schirmer, New York, n.d. A new synopsis and list of characters have been added, while the translated English texts within the work have appeared in previous Dover editions.

International Standard Book Number: 0-486-44953-X

Manufactured in the United States of America
Dover Publications, Inc., 31 East 2nd Street, Mineola, N.Y. 11501

Contents

Synopsis   ix
List of Characters   x

Introduction   1

Tableau I

The Enchanted Garden of Kastchei   3
Appearance of the Firebird, Pursued by Prince Ivan   4
Dance of the Firebird   8
Capture of the Firebird by Prince Ivan   12
The Firebird's Supplications   14
Appearance of the Thirteen Enchanted Princesses   20
The Princesses' Game with the Golden Apples   23
Sudden Appearance of Prince Ivan   28
Khorovod (Round Dance) of the Princesses   29
Daybreak   33
Prince Ivan Penetrates Kastchei's Palace   34
Magic Carillon, Appearance of Kastchei's Monster
    Guardians, and Capture of Prince Ivan   35
Arrival of Kastchei the Immortal, Dialogue of Kastchei and
    Prince Ivan, and Intercession of the Princesses   39
Appearance of the Firebird   43
Dance of Kastchei's Retinue, Enchanted by the Firebird   44
Infernal Dance of all Kastchei's Subjects   47
Lullaby (Firebird)   59
Kastchei's Awakening   61
Kastchei's Death   62
Profound Darkness   62

Tableau II

Disappearence of Kastchei's Palace and Magical Creations,
Return to Life of the Petrified Knights, and General Rejoicing   63

Synopsis

One beautiful day the Tsar's son, Prince Ivan, ventures off on a hunting trip. In the lush forest he comes across a fantastic bird with bright plumes of fire. Ivan carefully sets upon the bird and captures it. After some struggle, the bird pleads for its freedom, promising a magic feather in exchange. The prince releases the fiery bird and is a given a feather that will protect him from evil.

Ivan sets off into the forest once again where he comes upon an enchanted castle. In the courtyard there is a princess and 12 maidens playing in a garden of golden apples. After some hesitation, Ivan draws nearer and is allowed to join their game. As dawn approaches, the princess and maidens head back to the castle, warning Ivan not to follow–they are captives of the immortal Kastchei who turns intruders to stone. Ivan also learns that Kastchei's soul dwells not in his body, but is carefully preserved in a golden egg protected inside a casket. As long as his spirit is held there, Kastchei will not die.

Undaunted, Ivan enters the castle. He encounters rows of unfortunate victims turned into statues, triggers an alarm and is captured. As Kastchei prepares to transform him to stone, Ivan waves his magic feather. The Firebird appears, sending Kastchei and his entourage into a mad dance. Once they collapse, Ivan is freed and smashes the golden egg, killing Kastchei. The maidens are freed, the statues turn back into men, and Ivan wins the hand of the princess.

Characters

The Firebird
(L'Oiseau de Feu)

The Beautiful Princess
(La Belle Tsarévna)

Prince Ivan
(Ivan Tsarévich)

Kastchei the Immortal
(Kastcheï l'Immortel)

12 Enchanted Princesses
(Princesses enchantées)

Petrified Knights
(Chevaliers pétrifiés)

Adolescents

Katschei's Wives
(Femme de Kastcheï)

Indian Women
(Indiennes)

Katschei's Retinue
(Suite de Kastcheï)

Goblin's and Demons
(Kikimory, Bolibochki)

Two-headed Monsters

to *Andre Rimsky-Korsakov*

THE FIREBIRD

Introduction

Igor Stravinsky

TABLEAU I
The Enchanted Garden of Kastchei

Appearance of the Firebird, Pursued by Prince Ivan

3 **Allegro molto** ♩= 144

a) ⌐⌐ 6 ⌐ , etc.

Dance of the Firebird

Capture of the Firebird by Prince Ivan

13

a) switch hands

b) original rhythm: etc.

The Firebird's Supplications

a) alternate rhythm:

a) See note previous page.

Appearance of the Thirteen Enchanted Princesses

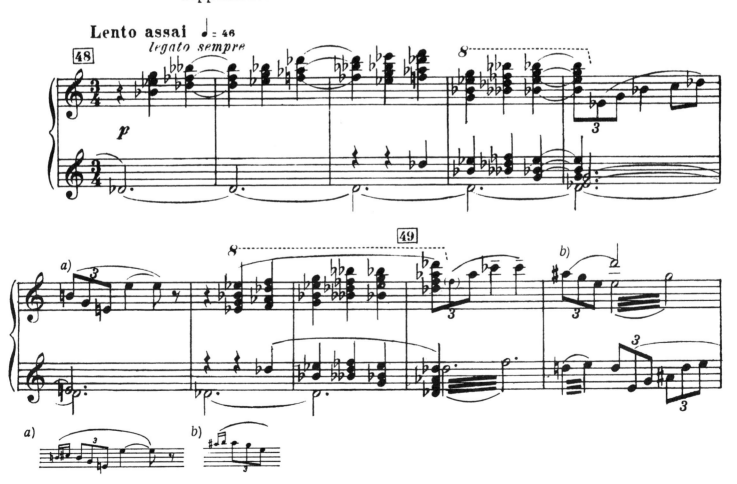

The Princesses' Game with the Golden Apples

SCHERZO

Sudden Appearance of Prince Ivan

a) In an earlier version, there were 2 empty measures preceding.

Khorovod (Round Dance) of the Princesses

Daybreak

Prince Ivan Penetrates Kastchei's Palace

Magic Carillon, Appearance of Kastchei's Monster Guardians, and Capture of Prince Ivan

a) See note, previous page.

b) Appoggiatura in tempo.

Arrival of Kastchei the Immortal, Dialogue of Kastchei and Prince Ivan, and

Intercession of the Princesses

Appearance of the Firebird

Dance of Kastchei's Retinue, Enchanted by the Firebird

a) ⊞⊞ etc.

Infernal Dance of all Kastchei's Subjects

a) Original rhythm: (γ) ♪ γ ♪ γ ♪ γ | etc.

Lullaby (Firebird)

Kastchei's Awakening

a) Original rhythm:

Kastchei's Death

Profound Darkness

TABLEAU II
Disappearance of Kastchei's Palace and Magical Creations,
Return to Life of the Petrified Knights, and General Rejoicing

Dover Piano and Keyboard Editions

Albeniz, Isaac, IBERIA AND ESPAÑA: Two Complete Works for Solo Piano. Spanish composer's greatest piano works in authoritative editions. Includes the popular "Tango." 192pp. 9 x 12.　0-486-25367-8

Bach, Johann Sebastian, COMPLETE KEYBOARD TRANSCRIPTIONS OF CONCERTOS BY BAROQUE COMPOSERS. Sixteen concertos by Vivaldi, Telemann and others, transcribed for solo keyboard instruments. Bach-Gesellschaft edition. 128pp. 9⅜ x 12¼.　0-486-25529-8

Bach, Johann Sebastian, COMPLETE PRELUDES AND FUGUES FOR ORGAN. All 25 of Bach's complete sets of preludes and fugues (i.e. compositions written as pairs), from the authoritative Bach-Gesellschaft edition. 168pp. 8⅜ x 11.　0-486-24816-X

Bach, Johann Sebastian, ITALIAN CONCERTO, CHROMATIC FANTASIA AND FUGUE AND OTHER WORKS FOR KEYBOARD. Sixteen of Bach's best-known, most-performed and most-recorded works for the keyboard, reproduced from the authoritative Bach-Gesellschaft edition. 112pp. 9 x 12.　0-486-25387-2

Bach, Johann Sebastian, KEYBOARD MUSIC. Bach-Gesellschaft edition. For harpsichord, piano, other keyboard instruments. English Suites, French Suites, Six Partitas, Goldberg Variations, Two-Part Inventions, Three-Part Sinfonias. 312pp. 8⅛ x 11.　0-486-22360-4

Bach, Johann Sebastian, ORGAN MUSIC. Bach-Gesellschaft edition. 93 works. 6 Trio Sonatas, German Organ Mass, Orgelbüchlein, Six Schubler Chorales, 18 Choral Preludes. 357pp. 8⅛ x 11.　0-486-22359-0

Bach, Johann Sebastian, TOCCATAS, FANTASIAS, PASSACAGLIA AND OTHER WORKS FOR ORGAN. Over 20 best-loved works including Toccata and Fugue in D Minor, BWV 565; Passacaglia and Fugue in C Minor, BWV 582, many more. Bach-Gesellschaft edition. 176pp. 9 x 12.　0-486-25403-8

Bach, Johann Sebastian, TWO- AND THREE-PART INVENTIONS. Reproduction of original autograph ms. Edited by Eric Simon. 62pp. 8⅛ x 11.　0-486-21982-8

Bach, Johann Sebastian, THE WELL-TEMPERED CLAVIER: Books I and II, Complete. All 48 preludes and fugues in all major and minor keys. Authoritative Bach-Gesellschaft edition. Explanation of ornaments in English, tempo indications, music corrections. 208pp. 9⅜ x 12¼.　0-486-24532-2

Bartók, Béla, PIANO MUSIC OF BÉLA BARTÓK, Series I. New, definitive Archive Edition incorporating composer's corrections. Includes *Funeral March* from *Kossuth, Fourteen Bagatelles,* Bartók's break to modernism. 167pp. 9 x 12. (Available in U.S. only)　0-486-24108-4

Bartók, Béla, PIANO MUSIC OF BÉLA BARTÓK, Series II. Second in the Archive Edition incorporating composer's corrections. 85 short pieces *For Children, Two Elegies, Two Romanian Dances,* etc. 192pp. 9 x 12. (Available in U.S. only)　0-486-24109-2

Beethoven, Ludwig van, BAGATELLES, RONDOS AND OTHER SHORTER WORKS FOR PIANO. Most popular and most performed shorter works, including Rondo a capriccio in G and Andante in F. Breitkopf & Härtel edition. 128pp. 9⅜ x 12¼.　0-486-25392-9

Beethoven, Ludwig van, COMPLETE PIANO SONATAS. All sonatas in fine Schenker edition, with fingering, analytical material. One of best modern editions. 615pp. 9 x 12. Two-vol. set.　0-486-23134-8, 0-486-23135-6

Beethoven, Ludwig van, COMPLETE VARIATIONS FOR SOLO PIANO, Ludwig van Beethoven. Contains all 21 sets of Beethoven's piano variations, including the extremely popular *Diabelli Variations, Op. 120.* 240pp. 9⅜ x 12¼.　0-486-25188-8

Beethoven, Ludwig van, BEETHOVEN MASTERPIECES FOR SOLO PIANO: 25 Works. Twenty-five popular pieces include the Sonata in C-sharp Minor, Op. 27, No. 2 ("Moonlight"); Sonata in D Minor, Op. 31, No. 2 ("Tempest"); 32 Variations in C Minor; Andante in F Major; Rondo Capriccio, Op. 129; Fantasia, Op. 77; and popular bagatelles, rondos, minuets, and other works. 160pp. 9 x 12.　0-486-43570-9

Blesh, Rudi (ed.), CLASSIC PIANO RAGS. Best ragtime music (1897–1922) by Scott Joplin, James Scott, Joseph F. Lamb, Tom Turpin, nine others. 364pp. 9 x 12. Introduction by Blesh.　0-486-20469-3

Brahms, Johannes, COMPLETE SHORTER WORKS FOR SOLO PIANO. All solo music not in other two volumes. Waltzes, Scherzo in E Flat Minor, Eight Pieces, Rhapsodies, Fantasies, Intermezzi, etc. Vienna Gesellschaft der Musikfreunde. 180pp. 9 x 12.　0-486-22651-4

Brahms, Johannes, COMPLETE SONATAS AND VARIATIONS FOR SOLO PIANO. All sonatas, five variations on themes from Schumann, Paganini, Handel, etc. Vienna Gesellschaft der Musikfreunde edition. 178pp. 9 x 12.　0-486-22650-6

Brahms, Johannes, COMPLETE TRANSCRIPTIONS, CADENZAS AND EXERCISES FOR SOLO PIANO. Vienna Gesellschaft der Musikfreunde edition, vol. 15. Studies after Chopin, Weber, Bach; gigues, sarabandes; 10 Hungarian dances, etc. 178pp. 9 x 12.　0-486-22652-2

Byrd, William, MY LADY NEVELLS BOOKE OF VIRGINAL MUSIC. 42 compositions in modern notation from 1591 ms. For any keyboard instrument. 245pp. 8⅛ x 11.　0-486-22246-2

Chopin, Frédéric, COMPLETE BALLADES, IMPROMPTUS AND SONATAS. The four Ballades, four Impromptus and three Sonatas. Authoritative Mikuli edition. 192pp. 9 x 12.　0-486-24164-5

Chopin, Frédéric, COMPLETE MAZURKAS, Frédéric Chopin. 51 best-loved compositions, reproduced directly from the authoritative Kistner edition edited by Carl Mikuli. 160pp. 9 x 12.　0-486-25548-4

Chopin, Frédéric, COMPLETE PRELUDES AND ETUDES FOR SOLO PIANO. All 25 Preludes and all 27 Etudes by greatest piano music composer. Authoritative Mikuli edition. 192pp. 9 x 12.　0-486-24052-5

Chopin, Frédéric, FANTASY IN F MINOR, BARCAROLLE, BERCEUSE AND OTHER WORKS FOR SOLO PIANO. 15 works, including one of the greatest of the Romantic period, the Fantasy in F Minor, Op. 49, reprinted from the authoritative German edition prepared by Chopin's student, Carl Mikuli. 224pp. 8⅜ x 11¼.　0-486-25950-1

Chopin, Frédéric, CHOPIN MASTERPIECES FOR SOLO PIANO: 46 Works. Includes Ballade No. 1 in G Minor, Berceuse, 3 ecossaises, 5 etudes, Fantaisie-Impromptu, Marche Funèbre, 8 mazurkas, 7 nocturnes, 3 polonaises, 9 preludes, Scherzo No. 2 in B-flat Minor, and 6 waltzes. Authoritative sources. 224pp. 9 x 12.　0-486-40150-2

Chopin, Frédéric, NOCTURNES AND POLONAISES. 20 *Nocturnes* and 11 *Polonaises* reproduced from the authoritative Mikuli edition for pianists, students, and musicologists. Commentary. 224pp. 9 x 12.　0-486-24564-0

Chopin, Frédéric, WALTZES AND SCHERZOS. All of the Scherzos and nearly all (20) of the Waltzes from the authoritative Mikuli edition. Editorial commentary. 160pp. 9 x 12.　0-486-24316-8

Cofone, Charles J. F. (ed.), ELIZABETH ROGERS HIR VIRGINALL BOOKE. All 112 pieces from noted 1656 manuscript, most never before published. Composers include Thomas Brewer, William Byrd, Orlando Gibbons, etc. Calligraphy by editor. 125pp. 9 x 12.　0-486-23138-0

Dover Piano and Keyboard Editions

Couperin, François, KEYBOARD WORKS/Series One: Ordres I–XIII; Series Two: Ordres XIV–XXVII and Miscellaneous Pieces. Over 200 pieces. Reproduced directly from edition prepared by Johannes Brahms and Friedrich Chrysander. Total of 496pp. 8⅛ x 11.
Series I: 0-486-25795-9; Series II: 0-486-25796-7

Debussy, Claude, COMPLETE PRELUDES, Books 1 and 2. 24 evocative works that reveal the essence of Debussy's genius for musical imagery, among them many of the composer's most famous piano compositions. Glossary of French terms. 128pp. 8⅜ x 11¼.   0-486-25970-6

Debussy, Claude, DEBUSSY MASTERPIECES FOR SOLO PIANO: 20 Works. From France's most innovative and influential composer–a rich compilation of works that include "Golliwogg's cakewalk," "Engulfed cathedral," "Clair de lune," and 17 others. 128pp. 9 x 12.   0-486-42425-1

Debussy, Claude, PIANO MUSIC 1888–1905. Deux Arabesques, Suite Bergamasque, Masques, first series of Images, etc. Nine others, in corrected editions. 175pp. 9⅜ x 12¼.   0-486-22771-5

Dvořák, Antonín, HUMORESQUES AND OTHER WORKS FOR SOLO PIANO. Humoresques, Op. 101, complete, Silhouettes, Op. 8, Poetic Tone Pictures, Theme with Variations, Op. 36, 4 Slavonic Dances, more. 160pp. 9 x 12.   0-486-28355-0

de Falla, Manuel, AMOR BRUJO AND EL SOMBRERO DE TRES PICOS FOR SOLO PIANO. With these two popular ballets, *El Amor Brujo* (Love, the Magician) and *El Sombrero de Tres Picos* (The Three-Cornered Hat), Falla brought the world's attention to the music of Spain. The composer himself made these arrangements of the complete ballets for piano solo. xii+132pp. 9 x 12.   0-486-44170-9

Fauré, Gabriel, COMPLETE PRELUDES, IMPROMPTUS AND VALSES-CAPRICES. Eighteen elegantly wrought piano works in authoritative editions. Only one-volume collection available. 144pp. 9 x 12. (Not available in France or Germany)   0-486-25789-4

Fauré, Gabriel, NOCTURNES AND BARCAROLLES FOR SOLO PIANO. 12 nocturnes and 12 barcarolles reprinted from authoritative French editions. 208pp. 9⅜ x 12¼. (Not available in France or Germany)   0-486-27955-3

Feofanov, Dmitry (ed.), RARE MASTERPIECES OF RUSSIAN PIANO MUSIC: Eleven Pieces by Glinka, Balakirev, Glazunov and Others. Glinka's *Prayer*, Balakirev's *Reverie*, Liapunov's *Transcendental Etude, Op. 11, No. 10,* and eight others–full, authoritative scores from Russian texts. 144pp. 9 x 12.   0-486-24659-0

Franck, César, ORGAN WORKS. Composer's best-known works for organ, including Six Pieces, Trois Pieces, and Trois Chorals. Oblong format for easy use at keyboard. Authoritative Durand edition. 208pp. 11⅜ x 8¼.   0-486-25517-4

Gottschalk, Louis M., PIANO MUSIC. 26 pieces (including covers) by early 19th-century American genius. "Bamboula," "The Banjo," other Creole, Negro-based material, through elegant salon music. 301pp. 9¼ x 12.   0-486-21683-7

Granados, Enrique, GOYESCAS, SPANISH DANCES AND OTHER WORKS FOR SOLO PIANO. Great Spanish composer's most admired, most performed suites for the piano, in definitive Spanish editions. 176pp. 9 x 12.   0-486-25481-X

Grieg, Edvard, COMPLETE LYRIC PIECES FOR PIANO. All 66 pieces from Grieg's ten sets of little mood pictures for piano, favorites of generations of pianists. 224pp. 9⅜ x 12¼.   0-486-26176-X

Handel, G. F., KEYBOARD WORKS FOR SOLO INSTRUMENTS. 35 neglected works from Handel's vast oeuvre, originally jotted down as improvisations. Includes Eight Great Suites, others. New sequence. 174pp. 9⅜ x 12¼.   0-486-24338-9

Haydn, Joseph, COMPLETE PIANO SONATAS. 52 sonatas reprinted from authoritative Breitkopf & Härtel edition. Extremely clear and readable; ample space for notes, analysis. 464pp. 9⅜ x 12¼.
Vol. I: 0-486-24726-0; Vol. II: 0-486-24727-9

Jasen, David A. (ed.), RAGTIME GEMS: Original Sheet Music for 25 Ragtime Classics. Includes original sheet music and covers for 25 rags, including three of Scott Joplin's finest: "Searchlight Rag," "Rose Leaf Rag," and "Fig Leaf Rag." 122pp. 9 x 12.   0-486-25248-5

Joplin, Scott, COMPLETE PIANO RAGS. All 38 piano rags by the acknowledged master of the form, reprinted from the publisher's original editions complete with sheet music covers. Introduction by David A. Jasen. 208pp. 9 x 12.   0-486-25807-6

Liszt, Franz, ANNÉES DE PÈLERINAGE, COMPLETE. Authoritative Russian edition of piano masterpieces: *Première Année (Suisse): Deuxième Année (Italie)* and *Venezia e Napoli; Troisième Année,* other related pieces. 288pp. 9⅜ x 12¼.   0-486-25627-8

Liszt, Franz, BEETHOVEN SYMPHONIES NOS. 6–9 TRANSCRIBED FOR SOLO PIANO. Includes Symphony No. 6 in F major, Op. 68, "Pastorale"; Symphony No. 7 in A major, Op. 92; Symphony No. 8 in F major, Op. 93; and Symphony No. 9 in D minor, Op. 125, "Choral." A memorable tribute from one musical genius to another. 224pp. 9 x 12.   0-486-41884-7

Liszt, Franz, COMPLETE ETUDES FOR SOLO PIANO, Series I: Including the Transcendental Etudes, edited by Busoni. Also includes Etude in 12 Exercises, 12 Grandes Etudes and Mazeppa. Breitkopf & Härtel edition. 272pp. 8⅜ x 11¼.   0-486-25815-7

Liszt, Franz, COMPLETE ETUDES FOR SOLO PIANO, Series II: Including the Paganini Etudes and Concert Etudes, edited by Busoni. Also includes Morceau de Salon, Ab Irato. Breitkopf & Härtel edition. 192pp. 8⅜ x 11¼.   0-486-25816-5

Liszt, Franz, COMPLETE HUNGARIAN RHAPSODIES FOR SOLO PIANO. All 19 Rhapsodies reproduced directly from authoritative Russian edition. All headings, footnotes translated to English. 224pp. 8⅜ x 11¼.   0-486-24744-9

Liszt, Franz, LISZT MASTERPIECES FOR SOLO PIANO: 13 Works. Masterworks by the supreme piano virtuoso of the 19th century: *Hungarian Rhapsody No. 2 in C-sharp minor, Consolation No. 3 in D-Flat major, Liebestraum No. 3 in A-flat major, La Campanella* (Paganini Etude No. 3), and nine others. 128pp. 9 x 12.   0-486-41379-9

Liszt, Franz, MEPHISTO WALTZ AND OTHER WORKS FOR SOLO PIANO. Rapsodie Espagnole, Liebesträume Nos. 1–3, Valse Oubliée No. 1, Nuages Gris, Polonaises Nos. 1 and 2, Grand Galop Chromatique, more. 192pp. 8⅜ x 11¼.   0-486-28147-7

Liszt, Franz, PIANO TRANSCRIPTIONS FROM FRENCH AND ITALIAN OPERAS. Virtuoso transformations of themes by Mozart, Verdi, Bellini, other masters, into unforgettable music for piano. Published in association with American Liszt Society. 247pp. 9 x 12.   0-486-24273-0

Maitland, J. Fuller, Squire, W. B. (eds.), THE FITZWILLIAM VIRGINAL BOOK. Famous early 17th-century collection of keyboard music, 300 works by Morley, Byrd, Bull, Gibbons, etc. Modern notation. Total of 938pp. 8⅜ x 11. Two-vol. set.   0-486-21068-5, 0-486-21069-3

Medtner, Nikolai, COMPLETE FAIRY TALES FOR SOLO PIANO. Thirty-eight complex, surprising pieces by an underrated Russian 20th-century Romantic whose music is more cerebral and harmonically adventurous than Rachmaninoff's. 272pp. 9 x 12. (Available in U.S. only)   0-486-41683-6

Available from your music dealer or write for free Music Catalog to
Dover Publications, Inc., Dept. MUBI, 31 East 2nd Street, Mineola, NY 11501
Visit us online at www.doverpublications.com